Simmered in Heaven

Angelic Healing Soups

(Hope in a Pot)

Created by
Angel in Aspen

Perfected by
two Fairies and an Elf

http://www.youtube.com/user/AngelicKitchen
http://www.youtube.com/user/AngelicLounge

Copyright © 2012 Angel Cusick
All Rights Reserved

No part of this book covered by the copyrights hereon may be reproduced or copied in any manner whatsoever without written permission, except in the case of brief quotations embodied in articles or reviews, where the source should be made clear.

ISBN: 1466337818
ISBN 13: 9781466337817

Disclaimer

Information provided in *Angelic Healing Soups* is neither intended nor implied to be a substitute for professional medical advice or to replace the services of a physician, nor does it constitute a doctor-angel-fairy-elf-patient relationship. You should not use information in this book or the information in the links from this book to diagnose or treat a health problem or disease without consulting with a qualified health-care provider. If you have or suspect you have an urgent medical problem, promptly contact a doctor. *Angelic Healing Soups* advises you to always seek the advice of a physician or other qualified health-care provider prior to starting any new treatment or with any questions you may have regarding a medical condition. Any application of the recommendations in these recipes is at the reader's discretion.

We also will not be held accountable for magical elixirs, love potions, or curses that go awry. Fairy Dust does wear out, so please check the expiration date so you do not turn into a toad.

*"Now to perform a true physician's part,
And show I am a perfect master of my art,
I will prescribe what diet you should use,
What food you ought to take,
And what refuse."*

— OVID OF ANCIENT ROME (43 BC)

Contents

Introduction — xi

Chef Bios — 1

Spandex Soup — 11
Weight loss
Loaded with vegetables from the garden, including cauliflower

Om Soup — 15
Vegetarian recovery soup that balances the system.
Squash and the Holy Trinity (onions, celery, bell peppers)

Love Potion — 19
Aphrodisiac
Apples, butternut squash, beets, and our secret weapon, pomegranate molasses

Oo-La-La French Onion Soup — 23
Antioxidant Soup known to cure all maladies
Onions, okra, green peppers, and celery

A Fairy and an Elf Cooking Classes on YouTube

Dharma Soup   29
Fights disease but not your karma, helps ulcers, regulates estrogen
Kale, carrots, leeks, cabbage, and a few other vegetables

Soldier Soup   33
Rare ability to raise antioxidant levels, fights stomach cancer
Peas, onions, carrots

Hippocrates Soup   37
The Definitive Soup to Fight Cancer, cleanse liver
Celery Root, parsnip, leeks, potatoes, onions, tomatoes

Meditation to Get Better   41
YouTube video to help the body fight any issue

Anti-Cancer Flush Apoptosis Soup   43
(causes cancer cells to commit suicide)
Lotus Root, astragalus root, kombu, green cabbage, kale, carrots

Suppa Duppa Chicken Noodle Soupa   47
Fights cold, immune boosting
Chicken, yellow onions, celery, carrots

Why the Strong Must Help the Weak   51
A Philosophy for Warriors

Sunshine Soup   53
Feel-good soup
Butternut Squash, Onion, Granny Smith apples, ginger

Do You Want a Reunion with Your Pet?   57
How to make contact

Downward Dog   61
Lowers blood pressure, hypertension and cholesterol
Red Potatoes, leeks, onions, spinach, lemons, garlic, lemon grass stalks

Energizing Water and Sacred Medicine   65
Secrets of the Elf and Fairies

Get Gorgeous   67
Antioxidants for youth
Apples, green tea, turnips, red onion, white onion, cabbage, carrots, butternut squash

Sour Flower Soup   71
    Mood-boosting soup
    Tomatoes and red peppers

The Chrysalis Stage   75
    Message from the Angelic Realm

Big Bad Bone Soup   81
    Bigger bones are always better
    Broccoli, bok choy, spinach

Creole Jumbo Gumbo   85
    Good for digestion, menstruation, and arthritis
    Chicken, sausage, onions, okra, green onions

Slouch Soup   89
    Energy for life
    Bananas, blueberries, honeydew, and other magical ingredients

How to Hear to Your Guardian Angel   93
    YouTube Meditation

Down The Rabbit Hole Soup   95
    Immunity boosting, improves eyesight
    Carrots, basil, ginger, and those devils even tossed in a cinnamon stick

Karma Soup   99
A Pistachio Delight, curbs appetite, antioxidant
Pistachios and multiple spices

Muscleiscious   103
Anti-Inflammatory soup for body and muscles
Potatoes, garlic and leeks, celery, watercress, onion

Doctor Harry's Happy Heart Soup   107
Give your heart a break
Pumpkin, black beans, onion, garlic, tomatoes, happy thoughts

Our Spiral Galaxy   111
The Little Blue Planet and its Connection to Eternity

Acknowledgment   113

Introduction

Look to the stars. We are all a part of their design, FOOTPRINTS left behind from STARDUST many LIGHT-YEARS away. Billions of years ago our planet was DELUVIAN, so a FULL MOON rising created mile-high tidal waves that crashed across the land. IMBEDDED in this land were mineral-rich NUTRIENTS that provided the perfect fertile structure for cellular interaction. *At the same TIME,* hurtling out of the sky were METEORITES that carried the building blocks of life (carbon) etched within their craggy backs. These silent blueprints slipped into the SEA—like PENNIES from HEAVEN—and VOILA! **PRIMORDIAL SOUP** was born.

We then grew into little fronds, gleefully floating in SWAMP WATER, and kept growing and evolving into something so MAGNIFICENT it can even have bad breath. If we were forced to swim in that SOUP now, however, many of us would probably drown or create more tidal waves. We have become, through all this stealth stellar interaction, completely Unfit. Disconnected. Lost in time. We need to look to our chemical composition for the answers. We are 96.2 percent chemicals that can be bought for less than a dollar in any chemistry shop. Add a zap of electricity and a few other minute elements and you have a MORTAL, capable of immense BRILLIANCE or brutality. We reside in a sort of celestial MOONSUIT that needs much more than the bad things we provide it. Our MECHANISM is otherworldly. It tries the best it can to do well in this primitive location, but it needs SUSTENANCE to make it whirl and spin or it will try to go back to the place from whence it came. These **Angelic Healing Soups** were designed to format this precise allocation, and were inspired themselves by something far, far away.

Chef Bios

The Angel

Angel (a.k.a. Angel C.) Cusick, part-time human and writer of this abstract soup book, has tattered wings from trying to help the Human Race, because she insisted on bringing some of Heaven's recipes down to Earth in order to make people feel better. There are many healing secrets in the divine kitchen hidden in the cellular structure of plants. Why did God hide miracles in plants? Because plants are not blabbermouths and can keep things hidden underground in the form of roots, leaves, seeds, and especially the bright, shiny fruits and vegetables beautiful to behold. Why did God wish to hide such important information? Because in Heaven he likes to play hide-and-seek with the Angels, so he thought humans would find it more fun to search for answers, too.

The body is a mechanism and the cogs that fix the machine all come from the natural world. God helps those who help themselves, and taking the time to concoct these magical soups will infuse healing deep into the cells, so that a part of Heaven will shine within you.

Angel comes from the furthest quadrants of the Universe, plus two Moons and a Star, and has been around forever. She comes every time someone asks her for help and loves when people help themselves through the *Angelic Healing Soups*. Sometimes she warps time to help your pain go away, and sometimes she makes birds sing to let you know she's there. She is the color in the butterfly's wing, and the glitter you see in the stars, but mostly she is that feeling you get deep inside when you know you've done something right. ASK for help and always give thanks, knowing that every murmur you utter gets heard in the furthest ports of Heaven, and, whether you realize it or not, you are never alone.

The Elf

Susan (codename: "Saggy the Elf") Saghatoleslami is an Imp who means business. As a teen in Elfville, she baked cakes and noodles, scoffing at the Fairy Queen who lost her cooking Crown to Sags and her magical soup wonders—some say—with questionable polka-dot mushrooms. Winning the Golden Wand for cooking, Sags got sick of hearing Fairies moaning because they didn't have their golden rod anymore, and decided to use common elf sense. She told them they could stick that Wand wherever they wanted IF they gave her their beloved Five-Star Stir-Fry Fairy Nectar Training. No Elf had ever been permitted into such a prestigious institution, which made those Fairies gasp in horror as they woefully relented. Being forced to get to know them, Sags realized there were some fierce renegade Fairies who taught her how to win slots in Vegas, and no Elves were as fun as that. Besides, it was much more entertaining watching them lose in foosball, football, snowboarding, golf, wakeboarding, and softball than squirting hot sauce on their wings. Sags reigns supreme as the Elf Champion of Cooking, and secretly likes to feed the homeless Fairies, who are always falling out of flowers. Sags denies being kind and caring as she runs for Elf President and keeps on whupping the Fairies' petunias in foosball and, of course, winning at slots.

Fairy #1

Mary (codename: "Sparklebell") Bright saves magic ponies and breeds baby dragons for the elite squad of Fairy Forces who fight cruelty to animals. Sparks turned her back on big Disney cartoons in order to take care of the fragile natural world. A sister to Tinkerbell, she learned how to create fairy dust from the deep, dark jungles of the Amazon. Sparkle can sprinkle fairy dust wherever creatures suffer, and Sparks loves to teach little children how to love and respect their pets since animals possess the most sacred secret of all—Angelic souls. Sparks puts her fairy dust into all her magic soups, and when people eat them, they suddenly want to help the less fortunate around them. Sparkle loves her baby dragons, and when they grow up, they're often seen coming over to visit and helping her start the fire to cook her soups. If you want to try her fairy dust, simply close your eyes when you are cooking and say, "Sparklebell, please make me well!" The dust will be invisible, but you will know it's there because you'll feel better—and maybe, if you look really good, a magic pony will fly across the sky or you'll begin to sprout wings.

Fairy #2

Bridget (codename: "Princess B") Balentine (formerly crowned "The Fairy Princess of New Orleans") has come a long way from being forced to shuck oysters on her thirteenth birthday. One summer's night, The Fairy Queen of Switzerland heard of her magical nectar from a flock of royal butterflies who had suffered tattered wings. The Queen, impressed that Royal B healed her butterfly troops, had them fly her in formation to L'Ecole d' Hotelier in Lausanne. Soon after, however, the Italian Fairies caught wind of her garlic broth and brought her to Florence to train with their gargantuan garlic wads. Sadly, however, soon after, the Pirate Fairies whisked her off to the Bahamas to be their galley chef for five whole years! It was here she found their sunken chest of cooking barnacles that utilize stars and moonbeams. Frightened at having to fly face down from the plank for finding such secrets, she escaped on the back of a giant squid who plopped her soggy wings smack dab in the center of New Orleans. Enchanted by the sound of song and dance, she stayed there for quite some time until fluttering up to snowy Aspen, Colorado. There her cooking dynasty began—but she still likes to wear an eye patch when she thinks no one is looking.

Spandex Soup

This organic soup was concocted to assist you in your efforts to find something FILLING, NUTRITIOUS, and YUMALISCIOUS. You will discover—even if you don't want to stop your incessant expanding—a craving for this kind of SUSTENANCE. Finally fulfilling the fantasy of your cellular structures, you may hear a strange voice calling out from the depths of your back closet. Your Spandex. Sad, neglected, ROLLED UP, and full of wrinkles, it will SPRING back to life the moment you stretch it back on, and you will suddenly have the URGE to go EXERCISE or do something else Healthy. SPANDEX, after all, is its own Reward.

Spandex Soup

1 large yellow onion, diced
1 bunch celery, diced (discard leafy parts)
10 carrots, peeled and diced
2 tablespoons olive oil for sauté
2 heads cauliflower (stalks removed and discarded), large chop
1½ tablespoons dried marjoram
16 cups chicken stock
2 pounds fresh spinach
1 bunch watercress
Salt and pepper to taste

Sauté onions, celery, and carrots in olive oil about 5 minutes.
Add cauliflower, marjoram, chicken stock—cook until veggies are tender, about 20 minutes.
Add spinach, watercress. Add salt and pepper to taste.
Puree with soup wand (I like a coarse puree; too fine gets like glue).
PGX Wafers are optional to eat with soup (not necessary, but add extreme satiation so you feel full).
Serves 6-8- or, sadly, in some instances 1.

Slinky and downright GROOVY ingredients include the following: PGX Wafers, plant fibers with APPETITE SUPPRESSING properties; CAULIFLOWER—CANCER FIGHTING, HORMONE-REGULATING, thought to particularly ward off Breast and Colon Cancer; SPINACH—CANCER FIGHTER, ANTIOXIDANT, Helps LOWER CHOLESTEROL; YELLOW and GREEN ONION—ANTI-INFLAMMATORY, Profound ANTIOXIDANT, ANTIVIRAL, ANTICANCER, THINS BLOOD, Lowers CHOLESTEROL, Warriors that together battle Blood Clots, Asthma, Chronic Bronchitis, Hay Fever, Diabetes, ATHEROSCLEROSIS, and Infections; CELERY—eight DIFFERENT ANTICANCER Compounds, Combats HIGH BLOOD PRESSURE, Mild Diuretic; CARROTS—a SUPERFOOD, ANIOXIDANT, IMMUNE BOOSTING, Prevents CATARACTS and MACULAR DEGENERATION, Lowers Stroke and LUNG Cancer risk, Helps with CHEST PAIN (ANGINA); and DRIED MARJORAM.

DISCLAIMER: Please note SPANDEX is a Privilege NOT a Right.

OM Soup

Breathe. Believe. Receive.

A recovery soup that cleanses the body, mind, heart, soul, and blood. Totally vegetarian, it infuses anti-inflammatory properties to help the system become balanced and pure. Using the "Holy Trinity" of cooking (onion, celery, and bell pepper), you will feel the healing rush through your veins. The chayote squash is a natural weight loss food because it contains tremendous amounts of fiber that fill you up. This soup also helps fight cancer, heart disease, cataracts, and inflammatory disorders such as arthritis and asthma. Soft, delicate, yet with incredible depth, this soup will wrap you in golden light and remind you that peace is only a few deep breaths away.

OM Soup

8 mirlitons (chayote squash), pale, green, soft, about the size of an avocado
1½ cups chopped onion
½ chopped celery heart
1 large chopped bell pepper
6 tablespoons butter or healthy margarine
4 teaspoons celery seed
2 teaspoons yellow mustard seed
4 teaspoons turmeric
4 teaspoons sage
4 teaspoons ground cardamom
Sesame oil

Par boil whole chayote squash (with skin) until tender, then, when cool, peel, seed and chop squash (also say this 10 times fast while you do it). Set aside 8 cups of the water you used to parboil the squash; this is now your veggie stock.

Sauté Trinity (onion, celery, bell pepper) in the butter (or healthy margarine like Smart Balance).

Sauté seasonings in a touch of sesame oil to release flavors.

Now sauté squash in Holy Trinity, and add seasonings with salt and pepper to taste.

Add squash stock 1 cup at a time and bring to a boil.

Serve while chanting, "Om Mani Padme Hum"—if you can handle the magic.

Serves 4-6 humble people

What is OM anyway?

Om is a mystical sound to be uttered before and after reading sacred texts, prayer, or meditation. Its vibration corresponds to a frequency of sound that opens the Crown Chakra (an energy porthole at the top of the head), which allows the white light of God to pour through. Try chanting this while making your soup, then ask God to Bless It and give Thanks for having something to eat. Notice how these "seed syllables" (Om Mani Padme Hum) transform your emotions into deep tranquility after only a few moments.

Love Potion

Do you want to be a good girl or a bad one? If you're good, are you really really good? Or when you're bad, are you better? Get Harps Strumming even if you do decide to take a Walk on the Wild Side (where Angels Fear to Tread). BE WARNED! May Induce Overwhelming Urge get devilishly Naughty.

Love Potion

- 3 cooked beets
- 3 large butternut squash
- 5 Granny Smith apples
- 10 cups chicken stock (or more if needed to cover squash and apples)
- 3-inch finger of ginger, finely grated, discard hairy fibers
- 7 tablespoons pomegranate molasses (Lebanese—find at specialty shops)
- 6 cardamom pods, smashed and soaked in ¼ cup hot water—use liquid, discard pods and seeds
- 6 tablespoons frozen orange juice concentrate
- Flavour to taste with nutmeg and/or ginseng

Cook beets by themselves, unpeeled, covered in boiling water about 45 minutes–1 hour. Peel when done and slice off discolored ends. Dice, peel, and seed butternut squash. Peel and seed apples, then dice. Cook beets, squash, and apples, covered, in chicken stock, adding ginger. When squash, apples, and beets are cooked (about 25 minutes), combine and add molasses, cardamom tea (water), and frozen OJ concentrate. Puree with a soup wand, or in a blender.

Approximately 20 cups Cupid would suggest

Triple X-Rated Organic Ingredients Include: Pomegranate concentrate, NATURAL APHRODISIAC dating back to King Solomon, who used it to lure women into his Pleasure Palace, where their images were carved into the walls (hoping to invoke FERTILITY), Vitamin C, B5, Potassium, Antioxidants and Punicalagins, which disseminates free-radical scavenging properties. REDUCES HEART DISEASE Risk Factors, including LDL, REDUCES OXIDATIVE STRESS, LOWERS BLOOD PRESSURE, Effectively FIGHTS Proliferation of Breast Cancer Cells in vitro, May have ANTIVIRAL and ANTIBACTERIAL effects Against Dental Plaque. Butternut squash totally loaded with Fiber, Vitamin C, Manganese, Magnesium, Potassium, and BUNDLES of Vitamin A. Beets reduce Blood Pressure and provide BORON, which produces Critical SEX HORMONES; Ginger, an APHRODISIAC that's ANTI-INFLAMMATORY, ANTIOXIDANT, and ANTIMICROBIAL and which HEATS the BODY UP, also is a STIMULANT (commonly referred to as "uppers") that produces a sense of EUPHORIA—counteracts Fatigue, Helps with FOCUS, and often SUPPRESSES the APPETITE so you can get more out of Your Dirty Weekend. Cardamom Pods (mild stimulant), Apples, Orange Stock—a Natural Stimulant that when blended with Ginger and Pomegranate becomes an APHRODISIAC. Nutmeg—a natural stimulant that produces MILD EUPHORIA in small doses, and a bit of

Ginseng that gives you the STAMINA to help you do you know what. Even if you're not looking for Romance, the Soup will satiate your need for something SUPER HEALTHY and FEELS SO DIVINE it'll make you think you have some DIRTY little SECRET.

OO-LA-LA French Onion Soup

People in New Orleans are of another world. Eating in the Big Easy is serious business, and their French Onion Soup can slow down time. The moment it enters your mouth, you are transported to a Victorian Era, where delicate flavors were blended together to create something so elegant, so dreamy, creamy, steamy, and delicious that nothing else will matter. You may seem in a daze as visions of naughty French maids concoct the soup for their masters—or innocent nuns scoop it up with their French baguettes. Either way, it'll put a smile on your face, and you may even hear your stomach shout out above the din, "Merci Beaucoup!" as suddenly YOU FEEL all OO-LA-LA inside. Open a bottle of wine. Drink.

Naughty—yet legal—ingredients include: Onions (reputed in Mesopotamia to cure virtually everything—anticancer agent—richest source of quercetin (potent antioxidant) —thins blood, lowers cholesterol—raises good HDL—wards off blood clots—fights asthma, chronic bronchitis, hay fever, diabetes, atherosclerosis, and infections. Also Anti-inflammatory, antibiotic, antiviral, and slightly sedative. Butter, flour, beef broth, bay leaves, thyme, and pepper.

OO-LA-LA French Onion Soup

4 large onions, chopped into crescents

6 tablespoons of butter

2 teaspoons of all-purpose flour

32 ounces beef broth, heated with 2 bay leaves

Salt and pepper to taste and serve

In a nice large pot (French maids like iron pots!), sauté the onions in the butter until they are brown or caramelized. Add flour, constantly stirring. Take another sip of wine. When the flour is cooked or smelling a bit nutty, add the heated stock a little at a time. Bring to boil and remove bay leaves.
Salt and pepper to taste.
Serves 6-8 people who should all be spanked.

If you're feeling a bit frisky, sprinkle in a little low-fat (shredded) Swiss, Gruyere, or dairy-free cheese. Serve with crusty bread and butter.

Keep glugging that wine until you look in the mirror and see this…

A Fairy and an Elf in the Kitchen
go to www.YouTube.com
Search for AngelicKitchen (one word)
Brace yourself.

Dharma Warrior Soup

A soup that fights disease, viruses, cancer, ulcers, and also regulates estrogen. Dharma is the all-around rock-'em-sock-'em soup that fights for law and order in your system.

Chock full of carotenoids, KALE has more beta carotene than spinach, and twice as much Lutein as any vegetable ever tested. Lutein, a little-known antioxidant, helps thwart breast cancer and also protects fragile lungs. Dharma soup is your hidden weapon that wipes out renegade forces even in your darkest nights.

Dharma Warrior Soup

- 3 medium leeks (cleaned and sliced)
- ½ bunch celery (¼-inch dice)
- 5 carrots (¼-inch dice)
- 3 cloves garlic (minced)
- 4 tablespoons olive oil
- 20 cups veggie stock
- 2 bunches kale (stemmed, sliced thin—Russian Kale is best if you can find it!)
- 1 bunch green onions (cleaned and diced)
- ½ head cabbage (sliced thin)
- 1 teaspoon thyme
- 2 teaspoons marjoram
- ¼ teaspoon ground cardamom
- 2 teaspoons fresh ground black pepper
- 1 tablespoon salt
- 2 teaspoons red wine vinegar

Sauté leeks, celery, and carrots in olive oil until translucent (about 10 minutes). Add garlic the last 5 minutes of sautéing. Add to veggie stock. Add sliced kale, green onions, cabbage, herbs, pepper, and salt. Cook until kale and carrots are tender (about 10 minutes). When finished, add vinegar.

Serves about 8-10 damsels in distress.

What does "Dharma" mean?

"Dharma" is a Sanskrit word that can mean several things depending upon the context. It's often used to mean "One's Righteous Path" but can also indicate a sustainer, supporter, and firm strengthener. Appearing in the *Upanishads* (ranked as one of the one hundred most influential books ever written), it's a representation of Universal Principles of Law, containing truth, order, and harmony that reflect the moral principles of the Universe. Dharma is truth and self-evident principles that go beyond all intellectual argument. The fabric that binds humanity. If you violate Dharma, you break Universal Law, and in so doing you destroy yourself

Soldier Soup
(Do we even realize what they gave us?)

Freedom is a word we take for granted. Most of the world doesn't have what we have, even in the "freer countries." We are always one generation away from losing our most precious right—and we don't even know it. In some countries, you can go to bed in a farmhouse your family has owned for hundreds of years, to awaken to horrific brutalities and armed soldiers taking away your home, innocence, and everything you've worked for all your life. There are two kinds of wars now—one that goes on in the killing fields and one that occurs in our economy, enslaving us to lower wages and a harder way of life. We must join forces NOW with our brothers and sisters in the field. It's critical to become the best we can be by educating ourselves and working towards a goal with something called "unconscious consciousness," which means we know, consciously and unconsciously, that we will achieve what we want. This is the secret to all success—and as we improve ourselves and learn new things, our mind expands to absorb its new reality. The universe spins miracles to propel us forward and does so in ways we can't even fathom. The soldiers make it possible for us to live in a free society where we are allowed to pursue our dreams—so know with every breath you take that the air was part of a country that many have died just for us to be in. "Carpe Diem" is Latin for, "go forth and seize the day." Why not go forth and seize your life? There are many soldiers who never got that chance, even though they had the same dreams, hope, and promise that you do today. Whatever you decide, be sure to send them a blessing and give thanks—they lost their whole world just for you.

Soldier Soup

2 onions, ½ heart of celery, 1 green bell pepper, all chopped (Holy Trinity)

1 cup chopped ham* (optional)

1 pound of dried green peas

18 medium carrots, peeled and chopped

5 charred garlic cloves

8 cups of cold water

Salt, pepper, and bay leaf

A one-pot soup that's cooked in a pressure cooker

Sautee Trinity. Add ham and rest of ingredients.
When using a pressure cooker, cook anything under 15 pounds for 30 minutes. Turn off until cool enough to open cooker—sizzling stops and pressure is gone.
Remove bay leaf, then puree.
Serve with a drizzle of parsley and infused or regular olive oil on top.
Serves 4-6

High in fiber and protein content, peas have an unusual combination of antioxidant and anti-inflammatory phytonutrients that turbocharge the capacities of any other vegetables added to them. They contain a unique assortment of health-protective phytonutrients that create their own little militia to fight disease in the body, as they provide platoons of fiber, lutein, protein, vitamins, and minerals that can battle any enemy invader. Peas also protect against stomach cancer.

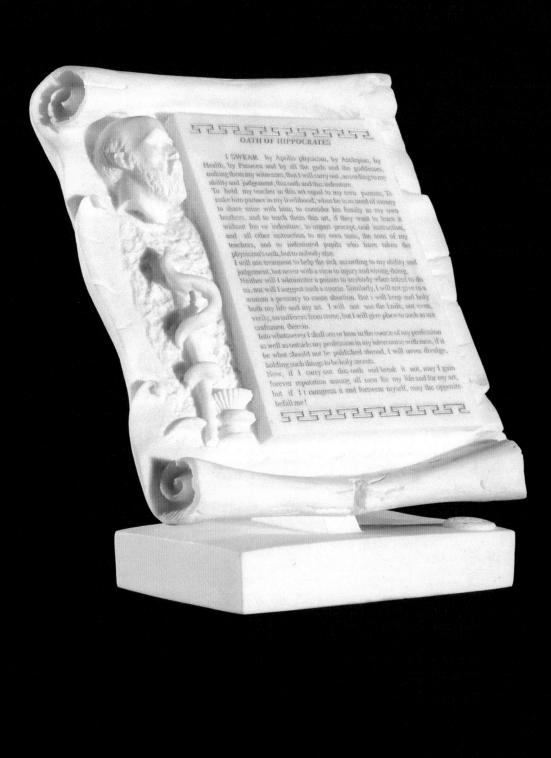

Hippocrates Soup

A 2,500-year-old Recipe Dispensed by LEADING Physicians even TODAY to Detoxify Kidneys, and Put Extra Zing in Your Wings. Fights ALL TYPES of Acute and Chronic Diseases, Aids in Digestion, CLEANSES the LIVER and has even been known to Heal Halos.

Profound Propensities Include: Celery (contains eight different ANTICANCER COMPOUNDS, Combats High Blood Pressure, Mild Diuretic); Parsley Root (ANTICANCER COMPOUND, ANTIOXIDANT, and Mild Diuretic); Leeks (Loaded with VITAMIN C); Tomatoes (ANTICANCER, Potent ANTIOXIDANT); Onions (ANTI-INFLAMMATORY, Profound ANTIOXIDANT, ANTIVIRAL, ANTICANCER, Thins Blood, Lowers Cholesterol, Raises Good type HDL, WARDS OFF BLOOD CLOTS, Fights Asthma, Chronic Bronchitis, Hay Fever, Diabetes, ATHEROSCEROSIS, and Infections); Potatoes (Anti-Cancer, Helps Prevent High Blood Pressure because it's LOADED with Potassium); Garlic (a WONDER DRUG that does everything you can possibly think of); Moonbeams; and Filtered Waterfalls from Secret Places…(we can't disclose the Whereabouts—otherwise we'd have to take you down).

Hippocrates Soup

1 celery root (can also be found in health food or Asian shops)

4 medium golden potatoes (about a pound)

1 medium parsnip

3 cloves garlic

2 medium yellow onions

2 small leeks

Filtered water to cover veggies

2 cans (28 ounces each) diced tomatoes, undrained (set 1½ cups aside for finishing the soup)

2 teaspoons salt

½ bunch parsley, finely chopped and set aside to finish soup (about 1 cup)

Peel celery root. Wash and scrub potatoes and parsnip, then coarsely dice celery root, potatoes, and parsnip in large pieces. Peel and smash garlic cloves. Peel and cut yellow onion in large dice. Cut leeks to the green part, cut in half, and clean really well under running water, then cut in large dice.

Cover all vegetables in water in a large pot. Add diced tomatoes with their juices, except for the 1½ cups that were set aside. Add salt. Simmer until tender, about 2 hours. Puree with a soup wand, then add the finely chopped parsley and reserved diced tomatoes.

Makes approximately 24 life-changing cups

Who was Hippocrates?

Hippocrates (460–370 BC) lived in Ancient Greece and was our Father of Modern-Day MEDICINE. He firmly believed DIET directly impacted health, and came up with this FAMOUS SOUP to COMBAT DISEASE, DIGESTIVE DISORDERS, and RAISE the IMMUNE SYSTEM by DETOXIFYING the LIVER. It is a soup that **fights all types of Acute and Chronic Diseases.** Now, the most sophisticated PHYSICIANS who lead the way in Science tell people to go home and eat Hippocrates Soup while taking their medicine!

Often, when I was young, there were these strange visions. Sometimes I thought it was God or an Angel or Saint who told me about "Divine Medicine." Everything seemed to operate through VIBRATIONS, and they taught me how the ESSENCE often had more impact than what presided in the real world. Most of the time I never really understood—as is the case here—until I got much older and was able to turn their words into wisdom.

When I was about nine years old, a man in a long brown robe came to teach me in a dream. He showed me a flower I'd never seen before that seemed to GLOW and SPIN, telling me it was called a "LOTUS FLOWER." Growing up in the Midwest, I'd never seen such a FLOWER. Then he showed me close-ups of its ROOT, explaining that it had some kind of "Medical Power" to cure cancer. I told the message to many grownups who just shook their heads and patted me on the back, asking me in hushed whispers if I'd "eaten any funny mushrooms."

New Studies are now coming out that have scientific documentation that the LOTUS ROOT does indeed transmit curative powers, one of which, of course, is ANTI-CANCER. We have concocted some truly mouth-watering SOUPS plumbed from the depths of deep reflection, SCIENCE, and ANCIENT WISDOM. We want to CHANGE the way you treat your MOONSUIT and make you aware that certain PHYTOCHEMICAL amalgamations (that is, certain plant-based foods put together) create a symbiosis that is so sophisticated we cannot understand it, but we know it helps the system reach a state of homeostasis, making it dramatically shrinks tumors and sometimes causing the body to go into a complete state of remission—if not cure.

*VISUALIZE pure white snow covering black rocks, and as you do, breathe in through the bottom of your feet. You may feel a slight pulsing or tingle—this is EARTH ENERGY, and it raises the immune system (among other things). Do this to remove any growths, tumors, cysts, lumps, anything you want *out* of your body (go to www.Youtube.com, search AngelicLounge (one word) and watch, *Accessing Earth Energy to Help You with Your Life* for further details).

Meditation to get Better
(whatever your ailment)

Anti-Cancer Flush Soup

Heaven-Sent Organic Soup That Will FLOOD your CELLS with LIGHT. Ancient Healing for the Broken Soul—or even the Happy Hearted—who wants something HEALTHY and DELICIOUS.

Propensities included are known to trigger APOPTOSIS—a natural healing process that CAUSES CANCER CELLS TO COMMIT SUICIDE. Lotus Root strengthens Blood, known to miraculously heal the Liver, Heart, Spleen, and Stomach. It also has high iron contents that help cure Anemia, INFUSE ENERGY because it's loaded with VITAMINS B and C, and also STOP all kinds of Internal Bleeding. Astragalus Root produces the most potent photochemical known to BOOST THE IMMUNE SYSTEM and SUPPORTS the ADRENALS to COMBAT FATIGUE and PROLONGED STRESS. It Increases Stamina and Remedies ANY immune deficiencies, including AIDS, Cancer and Tumors, and also Helps with CHRONIC LUNG WEAKNESS. Kombu is a Brown Algae packed with MINERALS that REMOVES RADIOACTIVE and OTHER TRACE METALS. Green Cabbage, an Anti-inflammatory that DETOXIFIES and CLEANSES CELLS, was also used by the Ancient Chinese to SHRINK TUMORS. Kale is an INTENSIVE ANTIOXIDANT and ANTI-INFLAMMATORY. Red Miso helps treat RADIATION SICKNESS and Provides a 50% BETTER CHANCE of FIGHTING CANCER. Carrots, Veggie Stock , Rice Wine Vinegar, Spring Water, and Lots of Angelic Vibrations to Help HEAL YOUR TATTERED WINGS. WARNING: YOU WILL GET SO HEALTHY, IT WILL OUTRAGE YOUR HEIRS!

Anti-Cancer Flush

2½ cups Lotus root, peeled and sliced thin, quartered

2 strips astragalus root

8 tablespoons red miso (1 small container) added to 16 cups veggie stock (I use Minor's dry and add to liquid)

6 carrots, peeled and sliced into thin rounds

1 bunch kale, cleaned well; remove stem and veins, slice leaves thin

1 whole piece Kombu, broken into small pieces before you add to soup

½ head green cabbage, sliced into ¼-inch strips about 2 inches long

Salt and pepper to taste

2 tablespoons rice wine vinegar

Soak Lotus root and astragalus separately: Soak Lotus root in water for ½ hour to make a tea. Break astragalus root and soak in ½ cup boiling water, off heat, for at least ½ hour; strain and reserve liquid.
To the miso and veggie broth, add soaked lotus root, carrots, kale, kombu, and cabbage.
Cook until veggies are tender, about ½–1 hour.
Add astragalus root tea, making sure to strain—you only want the tea.
Add rice wine vinegar
Season with salt and pepper
Makes approximately 20 butt-kickin' cups

Suppa Duppa Chicken Noodle Soupa

Loaded with Loving Thoughts from a Faraway place where Miracles are Spun and Home Delivered. Grandma's Soup always tasted best, and now that she's an ANGEL it's gotten even better!

Kind and Understanding Organic Propensities Include: Organic Chicken, Homemade Chicken Stock, Yellow Onions (your Grandpa used to like them) , Celery, Carrots, Italian Parsley, Green Onions, Astragalus Root (a tasteless herb that produces the MOST POTENT PHYTOCHEMICALS known to BOOST the IMMUNE SYSTEM and SUPPORT the ADRENALS to COMBAT FATIGUE and PROLONGED STRESS, Increase Stamina, and Remedy ANY Immune Deficiencies, including AIDS, CANCER, and Tumors, and also helps with CHRONIC LUNG WEAKNESS), other Healing Herbs, and a Little PECK on the Cheek just cuz she LOVES You.

Suppa Duppa Chicken Noodle Soupa

1½ yellow onions, diced

1 bunch celery, ¼-inch dice

8–10 carrots, peeled, ¼-inch dice

10 cups chicken stock

4 chicken breasts, boneless and skinless, 1-inch dice

5 chicken thighs, boneless and skinless, 1-inch dice

1 teaspoon each dried oregano, marjoram, sage, and thyme

2 bay leaves

2 strips (2 ounces) astragalus root* (optional), soaked in ½ cup hot water; drain and use the tea only

½ pound of rotini noodles

½ bunch Italian parsley

1 bunch green onions

1 teaspoon salt and ½ teaspoon fresh ground pepper

Sauté onion, celery, and carrots in olive oil.
Add chicken stock, diced chicken, and dried herbs and cook until veggies are tender and chicken is cooked, about ½ hour.
Take off heat and cool. Add all astragalus root tea, green onions and parsley to taste..

Cook noodles separately, cool, and add to soup once cooled (they will expand and absorb your liquid). If you are serving soup immediately, you can add noodles to the soup and boil until done, about 10 minutes.

Serves 6-8 annoying relatives who give her a headache every time they unexpectedly show up hungry and moaning.

Why the Strong Should Help the Weak

We are not all created equal, although we share one common denominator—the soul. Some souls come to Earth infused with wisdom, some need a knuckle sandwich, but most are sad, scared, or even broken, while many are confused over why they even had to come down here in the first place. We cannot always understand God's reasoning, but we can see quite clearly that most souls at some point need a little help—and the only one to help them is us. What better way to help them out than to make a nice, hot steaming pot of soup? Science doesn't always understand the secret world of plants, but the Fairies, Elves, and Angels do, and they have imparted some of their wisdom into these recipes, and if you really, truly believe, they will come to you in dreams. Just ask.

Sunshine Soup

In memory of Goldy, Ed, Mr. Saud, Cleopatra, and all other beloved pets who brought days of summer to our lives.

The ancient Egyptians believed all animals were divine because they exude pure, unadulterated emotion. Humans use their cerebral cortexes to process stimuli through the intellect—but our temporal lobe, where emotion gets processed, is small. Animals, on the other hand, have small cerebral cortexes for intellect—yet possess elongated temporal lobes, which is where the emotional world and all its secrets are totally understood. This means animals perceive the world on an **emotional scale** we could never begin to understand. *They know how we feel before we even know,* which is why they touch some deep inner chord within us that makes us love them so deeply.

So, in memory of all those beloved pets we've lost through time, this soup commemorates them. It looks like the Sunshine they brought into our lives, and the memories they left us we will never leave behind.

Sunshine Soup

1 large white onion (diced)

2 tablespoons olive oil (for sautéing)

4 cloves fresh garlic (minced)

3 inches fresh ginger (peeled and minced)

3 butternut squash (peeled and cubed)

5 Granny Smith apples (peeled, cored, and diced)

10 cups chicken stock (add more if you need to thin)

¼ teaspoon nutmeg

2 teaspoons sweet curry

Salt and pepper

Several drops of Saint John's Wort* or Bach Flower Rescue Remedy*

(*optional)

Sauté onion in olive oil until translucent, then add garlic and ginger and cook for 1 minute. Add cubed butternut squash, apples, and chicken stock, and cook until squash and apples are tender (about ½ hour). Add nutmeg, curry, salt, and pepper to taste. Thin with extra chicken stock if necessary. Puree with blender until smooth. Add drops of elixirs to each bowl. Give thanks for the time you had with your beloved pet—and send its soul a virtual treat.

Fills about 6-8 human or dog bowls

Ingredients in this soup can't wag their tail or lick your face, but they can lift your spirits and possibly help you lose some weight. Butternut Squash will fill you with fiber and flood you with Vitamins A and C, Manganese, Magnesium, and Potassium. The Granny Smith Apples are also high in fiber, which suppresses the appetite, reduces cholesterol, and has anti-cancer propensities. Ginger treats headache, nausea, and chest congestion, and as a natural anti-inflammatory also fights rheumatoid arthritis. Garlic and Onion are also ancient wonder foods that stop many maladies in their tracks—and together these potent ingredients create a calm and soothing elixir to calm the body and give a feeling of satiation. The Saint John's Wort is an invention from Ancient Rome to calm the nerves and lift the gloom. It too suppresses the appetite. If you want, you can also put a few drops of Bach Flower Rescue Remedy into the soup if going through a traumatic event. These natural remedies can be bought at any health food store and have been soothing people for countless decades.

with your Pet?

The ancients had a technique that can soothe the bereaved and give an alternate form of communication. Do you have his or her collar or some metallic object that he or she wore (such as a leash)? Hold the items in your hand as you go to bed, and ask God to surround you in White Light. Imagine a Violet Lotus Flower opening on the crown of your head. See an Indigo Blue Egyptian Eye opening on your forehead, and a Green Lotus Flower opening over your heart. Do not cross your arms or legs or twist your spine. Now breathe a White Light into your Crown (the Violet Flower) and out through your Third Eye, then in through your Crown and out through your Green Lotus Flower (heart). Now just go to sleep, breathing in through the Crown and out through the Third Eye and Heart. Once you hit the high vibrations, you will make contact.

It may occur immediately or take a few nights. The more you practice, the better it will become, and soon you will realize that your pet has really not gone away and has been there all along. Try to be aware of sensations as you fall asleep—you may feel your pet curl close beside you or lick your face or rub your leg. Try not to analyze events too much, since your pet will connect to you through the emotional body—not the intellectual mind. You may also find that pets speak to you through telepathy. Just be open to receive how they greet you—besides, they always knew what was best.

Downward Dog

A Soup that Lowers Blood Pressure, Hypertension, and Cholesterol

Potatoes, though looking dumb and cumbersome, are mini action heroes. Yes, they are dumpy little vegetables—and thank God they don't wear Spandex—but hidden in their mud-splotched skins are secret super powers the world so desperately needs. No, they do not have laser guns or x-ray vision, but something called POTASSIUM, a potent hypertension medicine that also LOWERS BLOOD PRESSURE in a single bound. SPINACH, its yummy sidekick, also tops the totem pole of potent foods. It helps fight cancer, morphs into an ANTIOXIDANT, and contains more BETA CAROTENE and three times more LUTEIN than broccoli! Rich in FIBER, it also LOWERS CHOLESTEROL. Crash! Bang! Wallop! to those nasty numbers your doctor keeps warning you about. GARLIC, a wonder drug since the dawn of civilization, also does all of the above and more, while ONIONS were reputed in Ancient Mesopotamia to cure virtually every issue under the sun. So, get the dogs in you to go down, while feeling calm, cool, and collected like an old dog who likes to sleep on the porch.

Downward Dog

4 red potatoes (scrubbed, *not* peeled)

4 large leeks

½ yellow onion

2 tablespoons butter (or Smart Balance Margarine)

2 lemon grass stalks, 4 inches (white part)

16 cups chicken stock

3 Kefir lime leaves (OPTIONAL! Hard to find!)

4 cups whole milk (skim is healthier, though)

2 cups heavy cream (this is a luxury—not essential, can be replaced by extra skim)

2 pounds spinach

Juice of 1 lemon

6 cloves garlic minced

1 teaspoon kosher coarse salt

1 teaspoon fresh ground pepper

½ bunch chopped Curly Parsley (about 1 cup)

Scrub potatoes—don't peel! Dice into large pieces and put in soup pan.
Cut leeks in half, clean well, and slice.
Dice onion and sauté in butter (or margarine) with garlic and leeks until translucent.
Add to soup pan.
Mince lemon grass (in blender works best), and add to soup.
Cover with chicken stock, add Kefir lime leaves and cook on MEDIUM BOIL until potatoes are tender. Remove and save 1½ cups potatoes to coarsely chop and finish soup with.
Remove Kefir lime leaves. Puree with soup wand.
Add milk, cream, spinach, lemon juice, salt, and pepper.
Finish with parsley and coarsely chopped potatoes.
Feel calmness pervade with each spoonful.

Serves 8-10 people with issues.

Energizing Water and Sacred Medicine

Most of these next few recipes come from Saggy the Elf, who only uses secret formulas muttered in Elf lore. The fact she parted with these magical potions is a testimony to the fact she has put away her pointy shoes to no longer use on wicked children. Now Sags wears a snowboard and can often be seen whooping it up on the mountainside, making wolves and grizzlies scatter, while renegade ice fairies join in as they make snow glitter in her wake.

Energizing water is a secret Elf trick to make it stronger for their magical brews. They also use Crystals and Flower Essences. Those all lumped together add a sacred vibration—but it's up to you to decide how far you want to take it.

Energizing water has been scientifically proven in molecular photography, with electron microscopes, and has been shown to change the structure on a quantum level, which enhances the effect of the water. Elves like to make quite naughty symbols to affix to their elixirs (e.g., warts, big bums, and stinky feet), but you can add positive images and affirmations (e.g., a big heart, pot of gold, or maybe a big pile of ice cream), scrawled on a piece of paper and put near the water. This is enhanced by surrounding with a crystal or two, and a few drops of fairy water—commonly known as Bach Flower Remedies, which can be picked up in any health food store. Why would an Elf have Fairy secrets? Because when it comes to Leprechauns, they have to team up! Those rotten Leps are always lobbing coins at them from their pots of gold under the rainbows—so the Elves and Fairies joined forces, getting way past their inner racial issues.

Fronds from the Ponds of the FOUNTAIN OF YOUTH:

Get Gorgeous Soup

GET EVEN with your MIRROR.

An organic SOUP created to maintain YOUTH by flooding the System with Antioxidants and other ingredients to keep your Electrons in Orbit. Be prepared for ADORATION and, sadly, jealous sneaking glances.

OUTRAGEOUS Propensities Include: Butternut Squash (loaded with Fiber, Vitamin C, Manganese, Magnesium, Potassium, and BUNDLES of Vitamin A), Onion, White Cabbage, Carrots, Turnips, Celery, Garlic, Lemon, Fennel, Kale, White Navy Beans, Red Apples, Green Tea (critical antioxidant transmitter that also helps the body absorb other nutrients), Spinach, Basil, Tarragon, Oregano, Thyme, Rosemary, White Pepper, and other BEAUTIFYING Agents to CLEANSE the SYSTEM and REJUVENATE THE SKIN. Imbues Flower Essences such as Crabapple, which helps RELEASE OBSESSIONS over some aspect of appearance or personality. WARNING: You may get TOO GORGEOUS and have to occasionally stick your head in the sand to avoid people gawking. Be Wary of growing conceit. Refrain from SIGNING AUTOGRAPHS!

(To energize water, place 10 cups of water in a clear container, place underneath the words "Love, Beauty, Youth, and Health" written on a piece of paper. Surround the container with Rose Quartz and Crystal Quartz.)

Boil:

20½ cups of water
2 red apples—leave the skin on, remove core and seeds, and chop in big chunks
1 green tea bag
3 cups butternut squash—cut in large pieces
2 medium/small turnips, about 3 cups—cut in a few large pieces
½ large red onion—cut in big chunks
2 cloves of garlic, cut in half
1 white cabbage—peel outer layers, cut out the stem, and quarter
8 carrots—peeled and cut in large chunks
4½ celery stalks—cut in large chunks
2 large chunks of fennel—golf ball size
Juice of 1 large lemon —about ¼ cup

After this mixture has boiled, strain the vegetables (dispose) from the broth. Put 5 chunks of the carrots and a few chunks of the butternut squash back into the broth mixture for flavor; however, they will be removed later. Return the broth to the stove.

Add to the broth:

3 cups kale leaves—finely chopped/shredded
2 tablespoons of garlic, diced
½ cup of thinly sliced and chopped red onion
3 cups spinach—finely chopped
¼ cup basil—chopped
¼ cup thinly sliced fennel (add this towards the end so some of the flavor remains)
¼ teaspoon thyme
½ tablespoon rosemary—stemmed and finely chopped
½ teaspoon sage
1 teaspoon white pepper

1 teaspoon sesame oil
2½ teaspoons kosher salt
¼ cup finely chopped fennel
After vegetables are cooked remove chunks of carrots and butternut squash.

Soaked overnight:
White Navy Beans—1 cup dry = 2 cups cooked
Boil navy beans and drain = 2 cups cooked.
Add to soup mixture.
Let cool and add:

Special Ingredients:
Bach Flower Remedies:
Rescue Remedy Bach Flower—add 8 drops.
Crabapple Bach Flower Remedy—add 8 drops.

Makes about 10 bootyliscious servings.

Sour Flower Soup

(Don't Be So Sour, Flower, I *might* let you out in a week!)

Flowers can be so moody, especially when you step on their stems. Elves get even more melancholy for a multitude of other reasons. Mainly, if there's no place to make mischief, they feel dejected, unloved, and misunderstood. Their mischief, however, has a higher purpose: to make the human race craaaazy, which slows them down from polluting the earth. They also get upset if their shoes aren't pointy, because in Elf Land the size of your point is EVERYTHING! So, they created a soup for cheering themselves up that's sweet and delicious, and often—when no one is looking—an extra tomato or two (or fifteen) can be lobbed at the evil sorcerers who are out in their gardens picking herbs for their wicked potions that hurt fairies and butterflies and all else that is true.

Sour Flower Soup

Tomato and Roasted Red Pepper Sweet Soup

(To energize water, place 12 cups of water in a clear container, and place underneath the words "Love, Peace, and Happiness" written on a piece of paper. Surround the container with Rose Quartz.)

Roast:
3–4 red bell peppers, about 1½ cups—peel the skin, seed, and chop. Set aside.

Boil:
12 cups of (energized) water, then add 8 large tomatoes or 18 small vine tomatoes.
Boil these until the skin starts to peel.
Remove and let cool slightly, drain the water, peel the skin, core and seed, and chop to equal 3 1/3 cups

In a new pan boil:
The prepped 3 1/3 cups tomatoes
2 cups low-fat chicken broth
¼ teaspoon salt
½ teaspoon pepper
½ teaspoon celery salt
Let cool slightly.

Saute:
¼ cup olive oil
½ white onion—chopped to equal 1 cup
½ cup basil—chopped
½ teaspoon toasted cumin
1 tablespoon garlic—chopped
1 tablespoon flax seed oil
Let cool slightly.

In a blender, puree roasted peppers and boiled mixture. Add the sautéed mixture, then add:
¼ cup cream
1 2/3 cups of low-fat chicken broth
Return mixture to a pan and heat to desired temperature.

Then add Special Ingredients—Bach Flower Remedies:
Aspen Bach Flower Remedy—add 3 drops.
Hornbeam Bach Flower Remedy—add 3 drops.
Gentian Bach Flower Remedy—add 3 drops.
Impatiens Bach Flower Remedy—add 3 drops.
Scleranthus Bach Flower Remedy—add 3 drops.

Makes about 6 sadistic servings.

The Chrysalis Stage

*To everything there is a season, and a time
to every purpose under the heaven.
A time to be born, and a time to die.*
—Ecclesiastes 3:1

It had been another gray, rainy day with lightning, thunderclouds, and bitter winds making one want to stay indoors, yet something kept telling me to go clear across London town to the lunchtime meditation at the college. Molly, an elderly medium, would conduct these biweekly sessions for virtually anyone who wanted to listen. Unlike the meticulous structures of the circles that maintained the same pupils sometimes for years on end, these informal sessions provided access to the public, and therefore always presented a cornucopia of odd personas. Due to the QUIET signs dangling from the bright brass doorknobs, and the fact that we never knew one another, there was seldom any interaction. Respectfully we would quietly file into the stillness of the calm, carpeted room and take a seat in one of the dozen or so chairs set up in a circle. At the designated time, Molly would walk in, take a seat, close her eyes, and begin to speak, and all you had to do was close your eyes and listen.

On this fateful day I was mad at myself for wasting so much time, wishing I had done a million other things that seemed much more important. I had piles of laundry, groceries to buy, people to call, studies to complete, post office chores, and stacks upon stacks of overdue library books to return, and if all that wasn't enough, I forgot my money and was starving. My active laziness (as the Buddhists call it) was busy spinning out of control, but it all melted away as Molly ever so gracefully waltzed into the room. Golden silence turned to respect as she sat down and gently gazed at us with wise old eyes, and suddenly I was so glad I was there. It was at this moment I noticed only three other people besides myself had showed up that day; an extremely overweight man, a young girl, and a middle-aged businesswoman. It struck me as odd since there were usually at least a dozen people present and often you couldn't find \Molly wore her hallmark dark blouse and trousers, with hair swept back and sensible flat shoes, looking more like an elegant lady from Harrods rather than some powerhouse medium. The only telltale sign of her distinguished profession was the antique crystal glass she wore around her neck. She put a pastille into her mouth, Angel.

There had been a tangible shift of the energy in the room that day as we all, save for Molly, suddenly opened our eyes. Although there was scant light from the storm raging outside and the intended lowered lighting, Molly seemed to suddenly glow in this bioluminescent white light. Her hoarse, sore throat seemed to completely disappear, as a young androgynous voice full of love and compassion radiantly flooded the room.

"Thank you for coming this splendid day. I come from what you call heaven or the Angelic Realm. You have all been summoned here to hear a special message." The Angel paused as we all waited breathless.

"We understand how hard your life seems to be. The loss sustained on this plane of awareness can seem cruel, the pain so hard to bear. Processing the death of a loved one can seem insurmountable and overwhelm even the strongest of characters. Grief comes in waves, crippling every moment, making day-to-day reality an absolute agony. Walls are erected, deflecting any consolation as the personality spirals deeper and deeper into depression, engulfed by a loss that defies comprehension.

"In these dark times, one must realize that the essence of the loved one still exists—even more vibrantly than ever before. It must be understood that the devastating loss of communication with the departed's physicality traumatizes the five senses because they are conditioned to see, feel, speak, smell, or hear only in the physical, three-dimensional reality. Finality to this process sends the senses into shock, as they reel in pain, overwhelmed by their inability to make contact—even though the departed's personality, in actuality, still exists just a heartbeat, just a vibration, away.

It becomes crucial now to turn inward to your sixth sense to make contact with this being, who is merely operating on a higher frequency and is still very much alive. Build the link to your conscious awareness to see that though on a higher vibration, they are still constantly around you. Quiet your mind and listen to your inner ear to that sound that comes in the arc of silence. Search the landscape of your dreams—that's usually where you'll find them

Try to make contact with the spirit you once got glimpses of when it had still been here on the Earth, and think of that twinkle you once saw in their eyes.

Think of the love they once showed you. Both of these are spirit. Love is the most powerful vibration in the universe. It is eternal and it's only a matter of time before any two souls reunite." (The Angel sounded almost tired of repeating this next phrase, as though it had been spoken a thousand times before). "**Yes**, we hear all your whispers, prayers, and tears; **yes,** we see all your deeds; **yes,** we feel all your joys and regrets. And **yes,** your departed loved ones hear you, too. Now train your sixth sense to feel the echo of their love, hear their whispers, see their smiles, smell their perfume, and, if you focus even deeper, you will hear your two souls laughing, and internally you will come to terms with the fact that they never really left you and had been there all along."

The Angel paused as we tried to compose ourselves and stop crying. It was as though it wasn't just our conscious selves crying, but as if our souls were crying, too. The words seemed to touch some responsive chord deep inside us as we all underwent this intensely deep catharsis on this most unexpected day. The Angel again began to speak as we desperately tried to digest and commit every word to memory.

"In spirit there is no time. But there is purpose to making things unfold in the right season and in sentience one must sometimes learn to go to sleep and await for this time to unfurl according to our heavenly chronometers—not your hurried human ones. If you try to rush things, you will be blocked and it will serve no purpose, except to disappoint and cause pain. There is necessary pain and unnecessary pain, and impatience invokes the unnecessary kind.

"All of you feel very alone at the moment. Spiritual evolution creates necessary pain facilitated by shocks, blocks, and disappointments that force false beliefs out of the psyche. It sometimes becomes necessary to take away beloved friends, family members, or things you counted on to experience this process, to reach new levels of awareness. It therefore becomes necessary to isolate the soul, and in order to do this, one must be put into what we refer to as **The Chrysalis Stage**.

"This process occurs the way an insect sleeps inside its cocoon, all alone, with no light or ability to move, before it slowly evolves into another creature entirely— one that no longer crawls on the ground through the muck and mire at the mercy of all other beasts, but finally, after a virtual death, sprouts wings, and can fly.

"This natural process is reproduced within your spiritual growth, although there is no shell to restrain you. Instead we use mental and emotional walls that serve the same purpose. These invisible prisons can seem harsh and very lonely, but once the lessons have been learned, the chains come off and life feels so much better than before. Every prison is different, but the end result feels all the same. Intense loneliness. It is at these times that slings and arrows seem to puncture your every move. Nothing goes right and people around you disappear, disappoint, or seem incredibly cruel. To help you comprehend this stage, we suggest you heighten awareness within your interactions with each individual. Notice not only who is speaking but what is speaking—often pride, sometimes malice, usually ignorance. Take account of these dynamics and see if there are any reoccurring patterns. If there are, learn how to process instead of merely reacting to them. Know that in time, this too shall pass, and ask your Guardian Angels for support. There are many in this room today, more than human beings, I might add" (the Angel chuckled).

"We know the Chrysalis Stage is difficult, but it becomes necessary to propel you forward to the next level. All loneliness ends when one is on the right journey, and kindred spirits will be sent along the way. If in doubt about the righteous path, ask for guidance. We relay all your messages to God. Every murmur fills our ears, we see every tear you shed, and even though you cannot feel it, we often kiss your cheek to calm you down and help you feel the love. We know life is hard. We know life is unfair. All this, we know.

"Look to help those less fortunate. In that gesture one will always, certainly find love and kindred souls on similar journeys. Helping others is God's path to inner peace and happiness. Love one another like your life depends on it, because in the end it does." There was a pause as the Angel's words fell deep inside our souls.

"Peace be with you all."

And then our Angel was gone, but we felt so blessed that such a glorious being had momentarily graced our lives. Mere words cannot define the feeling we experienced in the room that day listening to the Angel. When Molly came to, she seemed disoriented, like coming out of a deep sleep. She told us it was a momentous day and nothing like that had ever happened to her before. She calmly got up and left the room as the four of us compared notes, and indeed it was true, we were all going through the Chrysalis Stage and had recently lost loved ones and were feeling so alone. Finally, upon leaving the college, we were surprised to greet sunshine and find the dark skies had turned a bright cornflower blue. I sat down in a beam of light on the steps and scrawled these words in a small spiral notebook, hoping one day to repeat them to somebody else.

An authentic testimony found inside THE PSYCHOLOGY OF THE SOUL,
By: Angel Cusick

Big Bad Bone Soup

Sometimes Elves break bones from all the extreme sports they like to play. The Fairies like to egg them on and just wave a magic wand to fix them when things get too out of hand. The Elf mothers, however, want their little Elvinas and Elvinos to be strong—especially if they're attacked by flying monkeys or the occasional lawn mower.

Big Bad Bone Soup

(To energize water, place 16 cups of water in a clear container, place underneath the words "Love, Well Balanced, Strength, and Solid" written on a piece of paper, and surround the container with Rose Quartz, Calcite, and Iron Pyrite.)

Boil:
16 cups of water
4 cups broccoli—chopped
2 cups Bok Choy green leaves—chopped
2 cups spinach—stemmed and slightly chop
Let cool slightly.

Saute:
¼ cup olive oil
2 ½ tablespoons garlic—diced
1 cup scallions—sliced thin
2/3 cup white onion—chopped
2 cups spinach—slightly chopped
2 cups Bok Choy (the white part)—chopped
½ tablespoons dill
½ tablespoons pepper
1 teaspoon salt
Let cool slighIn a blender, puree the boiled mixture with the sautéed mixture. Add ½ cup low-fat milk and 1½ cups organic chicken broth.

Return to pot on low heat and slowly add:
½ cup white cheddar cheese—finely grated
1 cup parmesan cheese—finely grated
Let cool slightly and fold in:
½ cup half-and-half
Turn off the heat.

In a clean sauté pan, sauté:
2 tablespoons olive oil
4 cups spinach—slightly chopped
Drain off oil, then fold spinach into the soup mixture, heat to desired temperature, and add:

Special Ingredients:
Bach Flower Remedies:
Olive Bach Flower Remedy—add 6 drops.
Walnut Bach Flower Remedy—add 6 drops.

Reasons for choosing these foods and spices:
The foods chosen for this recipe are high in calcium and magnesium. Magnesium is also needed to help absorb the calcium. Both calcium and magnesium are needed to help the body strengthen bones and tissue and are also very helpful for repairing broken bones.

Makes about 6 servings.

Creole Jumbo Gumbo

The Louisiana Secret

Louisiana is a secret place where time stands still—even when stomachs don't. Through the port, where many cultures came hoping to find a New World, people brought, along with their dreams and prayers, secret spices and recipes so sacred that they actually named the essence of it the Holy Trinity (onion, celery, and green bell peppers). Considered the most delicious food in all the land, Creole cooking blends the best of French, African, Spanish, and Haitian cuisine. Add a roux to create a nutty flavor, along with bay leaf, Andouille Sausage, Tasso (cured ham), okra (an African vegetable), and the filĕ (sassafras), and voila! You have a healing gumbo—not packed with mumbo-jumbo—but miniature worlds where people's love of the earth and the sky can actually be tasted.

Ssshhhh! These secret ingredients also aid in digestion, menstruation, and arthritis, and they are anti-inflammatory.

Creole Jumbo Gumbo

1 large tender chicken (the biggest sucker you can find)

4 bay leaves, thyme, salt, cayenne pepper, black pepper, oregano, parsley, all to taste!

1 pound Andouille sausage (or any smoked sausage), cut into rings

3 tablespoons butter or oil

½ cup all-purpose flour

2 large onions, 1 celery bunch, 2 green bell peppers, all chopped and set aside

1 pint of okra, sliced into ½-inch pieces

1 bunch green onions, chopped

File powder, optional

Hot Sauce, to finish

Place chicken in a large stock pot with cold water. Add 2 of the 4 bay leaves and salt. Boil until tender, then remove from stock and cool. Cut chicken into pieces (no bones).
Heat a cast iron skillet and sauté the sausages over medium heat until brown. Drain on paper towels.

In that heavy iron skillet, prepare a roux! Heat butter or oil on medium setting and sprinkle flour in, stirring constantly! At this point the true meditation begins—because you are gonna stir that roux for a long time to get the dark amber color. This is the most important part, because herein lies the base you build upon.

It will be extremely hot, so be careful never to touch the roux. You burn it and you start over. Be proud of your foundation.
Carefully add the chopped onions, then bell peppers, then celery, stirring constantly and really watching so you don't burn yourself on

the steam. Stir in the okra; stir for a moment. No scorching. Add the chicken and sausage and stir well.

Slowly add heated stock and stir well. Then add your seasonings—salt, pepper, thyme, bay leaves, oregano, and parsley. Cook over medium to low heat for about an hour.

If a cannibalistic merman is calling, you can add shrimp and/or oysters at this time. Cook another few minutes and turn off. Just before serving, add green onions, then file. You should not add the file while boiling or reheat the gumbo once the file is added (could make it stringy) Remove bay leaves prior to serving.

Serve over cooked rice, with hot, crusty bread and butter!
Should serve 10-12 revellers.

African- Creole-New-Orleanian, this is a soup for reconnection to the earth or root chakra by using the okra, file (sassafras root), and of course the Holy Trinity of cooking (onions, celery, and bell pepper). Judge the amount of Hot Red Cayenne by exactly how much you wish to open the experience! Don't be in a hurry here; this one should take some time—because that's how we roll in the "Big Easy."

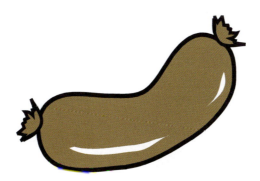

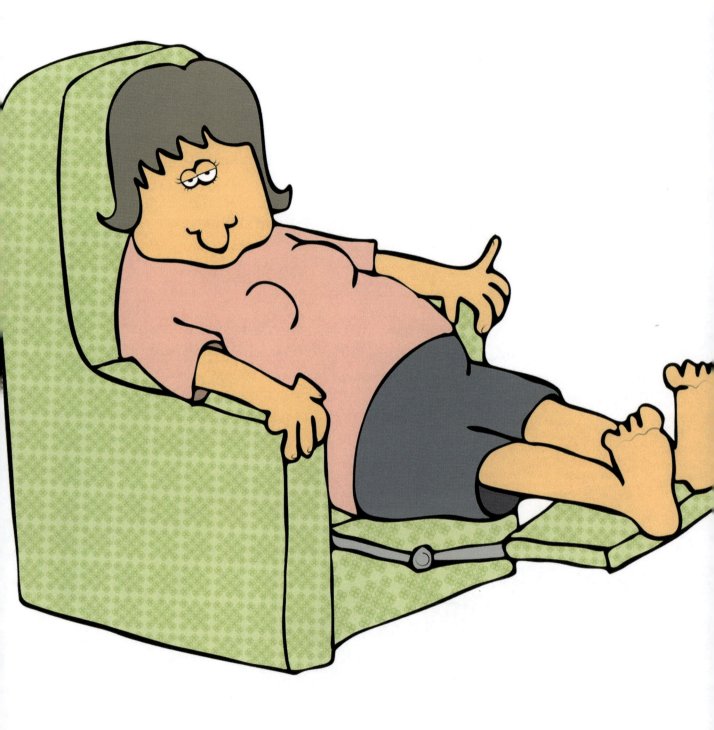

Slouch Soup

(An Elf Energy Soup)

We all have a little slouch in each of us. Elves especially like to watch foosball on TV and play video games, when they should be out in the forest helping snails with their trails, teaching reindeer how to fly, and showing wolves how to howl at the moon. This soup is a great way to get you out of your armchair and make you feel like you're part of this mysterious thing we call life.

Slouch Soup

Blueberry and Banana and Honeydew (maybe served cold or hot)

Water is energized with: Energy and Strength with a Quartz Crystal
(To energize water place ½ cup of water in a clear container, place underneath the words "Energy and Strength" written on a piece of paper, and surround the container with Crystal Quartz.)

Prep:
½ cup banana, chopped in medium pieces
½ cup blueberries, washed
1 cup honeydew or cantaloupe melon, chopped in medium cubes
Purée these ingredients in a blender and then add to and puree:
1 teaspoon flaxseed oil
1 tablespoon flaxseed—ground
¼ teaspoon cinnamon
¼ teaspoon vanilla extract
½ cup energized water (see above; this should be done ahead of time and the water can energize while other ingredients are being prepped)

Then add Special Ingredients—Bach Flower Remedies:
Walnut Bach Flower Remedy—2 drops
Olive Bach Flower Remedy—2 drops

To serve cold, pour into a bowl and add on top:
1/8 cup slivered or sliced almonds (for a crunchier taste, use slivered almonds, and for a more delicate taste, use the sliced almonds)
Another option could be to add 1/8 cup of granola if desired.
To serve hot, pour the above mixture into a sauce pan and heat. Then pour into a bowl and add the almonds (and/or granola).

Serves 4 couch potatoes

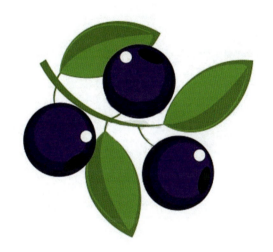

How to Hear Your Guardian Angel

YouTube Meditation
Go to www.YouTube.com,
and search for:
AngelicLounge (one word) and watch

HOW TO MEET YOUR GUARDIAN ANGEL

(look for the pink wings).

Down the Rabbit Hole Soup

(Immunity Booster made with Carrots and Ginger)

Have you ever wondered how rabbits can hop so fast yet have never ever been seen even once wearing glasses? Saggy pondered this great mystery of the Universe, so she went down a rabbit hole to spy on a bunny family with forty-two kids! When they were all getting ready for bed, she snuck into their pantry and found the recipe to this ever-confounding question. The rabbit race isn't happy their secret is out, so next time you see one, give it a high five, throw it a few carrots, or just run like greased lightning the other way.

Down the Rabbit Hole Soup

(To energize water, place 10 cups of water in a clear container, place underneath the words "Love, Health, and Strength" written on a piece of paper, and surround the container with Rose Quartz and Amethyst.)

Boil:
10 cups of energized water
8 cups thickly chopped carrots
4 chunks of ginger—peeled, cut to 1½ inches long
½ cup basil—lightly chopped
1 large or 2 small cinnamon sticks

Remove cinnamon stick and chunks of ginger. Strain the carrot mixture from the water. Set the water aside.
Chop 1 tablespoon of the ginger and add back into the carrots.
Let cool slightly and set aside.

Saute:

¼ cup olive oil
2/3 cup white onion—diced
1 cup celery—diced
1 tablespoon and 1 teaspoon garlic—diced
½ teaspoon anise seed—crushed
½ teaspoon cinnamon plus 1/8 teaspoon cinnamon
½ teaspoon nutmeg plus 1/8 teaspoon nutmeg
1/8 teaspoon powdered ginger
½ teaspoon lemon pepper
¼ teaspoon mustard seed—crushed
½ tablespoon rosemary—stemmed and finely chopped
½ tablespoon thyme—stemmed
1 tablespoon and 2 teaspoons of orange zest

Let cool slightly.

In a Blender, puree carrot mixture and add the sautéed mixture. (When pureeing the mixtures, if a creamier soup is desired, puree more; if chunkier soup is desired, puree less.)

Put back in a pot, heat, and add:

Fresh squeezed orange juice—2 large oranges to equal ¾ cup
4½ cups of the carrot broth set aside earlier
½ cup water
1 cup chicken broth
1 teaspoon salt

Let Cool and Add Special Ingredients:

Bach Flower Remedies
Rescue Remedy Bach Flower—add 4 drops.
Crabapple Bach Flower Remedy—add 4 drops.
Olive Bach Flower Remedy—add 4 drops.

Makes about 6 rabbits thump their paws (you may have to use pepper spray while dining)

Karma Soup

We all emit energy, a magnetic frequency that either attracts or repels everything—depending upon intent—into our daily life. It's important, actually imperative, to have positive thoughts, intents, words, and deeds. Everything you do is registered, and that creates an aggregate energy, which can make or break a life. In this spirit, we've concocted a soup that vibrates with so much positive energy, its authentic name, "Pistachio Delight," will fluff your pillows—and even make you forgive that little vixen Eve.

Pistachios are full of antioxidants, which are great for helping to prevent cell damage. In a USDA study, pistachios were placed in the group with the highest antioxidant capacity, as compared to over one hundred different foods. Pistachios have a significant amount of protein, healthy fat, and dietary fiber, all three of which can increase your feeling of fullness and the length of time it takes to get hungry again. When you're feeling full, you tend to eat less throughout the day, which can lead to weight loss. Even savoring a snack of thirty pistachios (about one hundred calories) may be enough to curb your appetite when hunger strikes- (but please save the frolicking around in a loin cloth for your next life).

Prep:

3 cups of canned Pistachio (salted)—ground in blender
2 cups of energized veggie broth
2 cups of energized water
Put in a pot on low heat and mix together.

Saute:

3 tablespoons olive oil
1 2/3 cups finely chopped leeks
¼ cup white onion, finely chopped
1 tablespoon and 1 teaspoon garlic, finely diced
1 teaspoon grated ginger
1 teaspoon cumin powder (toasted)
½ teaspoon turmeric
1¼ teaspoons garam masala spice
1/8 teaspoon pepper
Add to pistachio mixture in the pot on the stove.

Then add:

3 cups of energized veggie broth
3 cups of energized water
1 cup fresh squeezed orange juice

Saute with a little of the soup mixture:

2 cups of tofu cut in small chunks
3 tablespoons chopped scallions
Then add to the soup mixture and heat to desired temperature.

Then add Special Ingredients—Bach Flower Remedies:

Rescue Remedy Bach Flower—4 drops
Honeysuckle Bach Flower—4 drops
Chestnut Bud Bach Flower—4 drops
Makes 6 Sinful Servings

What is Karma, You Ask?

It's an innate equalizing force in the Universe, where no bad deed goes unpunished—and no good deed goes unrewarded. In other words, what you sow, you reap. There's a clincher, however, that I'm going to fill you in on. If you do something bad and you're a thick-head (primate), you will have to pay about three times for what you did wrong. So, if you steal a muffin that costs .89¢, it'll cost you about $2.67 in some way within the next few days. If you are highly evolved, but still cannot resist the call of said muffin, you will have to pay between seven and ten times for your "penance," anywhere from $6.23 to $8.90—and it will occur at the worst time you can think of. Now, if you're doing good deeds, but you're kind of a ding-dong, have smelly breath, and are an annoying kind of person, BUT you donate $5.00 to the muffin society, it will come back to you times ten ($50.00). However, as an evolver in training, it will pay you back maybe three times over ($15.00). Why, you ask, then SHRIEK, is the Universe so unfair? *Because it wants us to do it for nothing*. When we get to a place where we give because we want to **help out**, the Universe sends us gobs and gobs of good things—and all we want to do when we get them is give them to somebody else.

Muscleiscious

(A Potato Garlic Leek Soup)

Do your MUSCLES ACHE? Do you feel as TUCKERED as a Tadpole? You probably suffer from INFLAMMATION and need to ALKALINIZE your System. OVERWORKED MUSCLES and JOINTS need SUSTENANCE to recover; otherwise, Pain sets in and you have no more desire to SlamDance—or even do the Funky Chicken. BEHOLD! The Sacred Disco Ball Awaits!

Muscleiscious

(The ingredients chosen for this soup have anti-inflammatory properties and help to rejuvenate the muscles.)

Boil:

3 cups of organic fat-free chicken broth
8 cups of energized water
5 potatoes, chopped in chunks (7 cups)-
1 whole cucumber, peeled
2 small sticks lemon grass
6 medium to large cloves garlic, cut in half

After potatoes are done cooking, drain. Take out the cucumber, cut lengthwise in quarters, and seed. Remove the garlic and set aside with the cucumber. Remove lemon grass sticks and let the mixture cool slightly.

Saute:

¼ cup olive oil
3 small leeks—sliced thin and cut in half to equal 2 cups
2 cloves garlic to equal 1 tablespoon diced
7 ounces chicken broth
½ medium white onion to equal 1 cup cubed
11/3 cup celery—diced
¼ teaspoon celery seed—crushed
2 tablespoons apple cider vinegar
3 tablespoons parsley—finely chopped
1 teaspoon watercress—finely chopped
1 teawspoon white pepper
¼ teaspoon salt
Saute above ingredients and let cool slightly.

In a blender, puree sautéed mixture, then add the cucumber and garlic from the boiled mixture. Add 21 ounces of fat-free organic chicken broth, ½ cup of cream, and ¾ teaspoon of salt. Add the potatoes, using the pulse setting on the blender so that the potatoes remain in small chunks, then remove from blender. Fold in 20½ ounces of fat-free organic chicken broth and ½ cup of cream.
(If a smoother version is desired, puree potatoes to desired consistency.)

Special Ingredients—Bach Flower Remedies:

Olive Bach Flower Remedy (strength)—6 drops
Walnut Bach Flower Remedy (protection)—6 drops

(To energize water, put 8 cups of water in a clear container, then place underneath the words "Strength and Power" written on a piece of paper. Surround the container with Turquoise and Smokey Quartz.)

Makes about 10 mighty servings

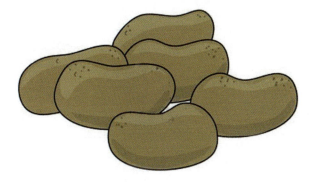

DOCTOR Harry's Happy HEART SOUP

This Soup cleanses the HEART, because pumpkins, rich in carotenoids, are efficient free-radical scavengers. Humans and animals are incapable of synthesizing carotenoids (RATS!), so they must obtain them through their diet. Carotenoids are powerful antioxidants—antioxidants are the good guys that keep the free radicals from knocking our electrons out of orbit. When our electrons are out of orbit, we age, disease sets in, and we live a compromised life. Though a vegetarian soup, it's loaded with a bucket full of protein and fiber and all sorts of weird and wonderful phytochemicals sent from Heaven's gate to fill your heart with intense health. No wonder that pumpkin scowls—'cuz he knows we're going to eat him!

Doctor Harry's Happy Heart Soup

1¼ onions, chopped

4 to 5 garlic cloves, minced

½ tablespoon canola oil

Black pepper to taste

3 (15-ounce) cans organic black soybeans or other black beans

1 (28-ounce) can no-salt tomatoes

1 (32-ounce) carton vegetable broth

1 (15-ounce) can pumpkin

2 Southwest black bean burgers (or other soy burger), chopped

5 heaping tablespoons GROUND flaxseed (by already ground or use a coffee bean grinder)

Yummy, dreamy, creamy horseradish for garnish

Sauté the onion and garlic in the oil until onions are translucent. Add black pepper. Stir in beans, tomatoes, broth, pumpkin, and chopped black bean burgers and that healing ingredient flaxseed. Simmer uncovered for 25 minutes, until thickened. Garnish with the creamy horseradish. Make a wish for a happy heart. Serves 6–8.
Can be served with hearty whole-grain bread.
*The secret weapon, flaxseed, contains fiber and phytochemicals and is loaded with omega-3 fatty acids—something the heart loves.

We live in a *spiral galaxy*, which often becomes replicated on the Earth. Everything from the sprigs of a grapevine's tentacle to a snail's shell and our own DNA serves to remind us from what we came—and how to get back there.

Spirals are like motion in a static state, and we are seemingly static but are really in a **state of motion**. What gives us our locomotion is thought, because what we create deep inside of our minds becomes our reality— be it a **HEAVEN** or a hell.

The food we eat can either launch our bodies and our minds upwards or send them spiraling down. We are each a symphony of sounds and oscillations, heartbeats, brain waves, pulses, breath, and other syncopations that serve to remind us that we are indeed alive. We are the microcosm of the macrocosm, and we need elements of the natural world in order to connect us back to ourselves. We must thus feed our energetic constitutions the proper vibratory food needed to stay healthy, repair damage—or just feel vibrantly alive.

These **Angelic Healing Soups** were inspired to RAISE your vibration, and shift you to a place where healing will occur.. There are many moons in HEAVEN, and these soups were brought down on a wing and a prayer through their light. After eating them, you will feel different inside, and upon awakening, listen carefully—for you may hear the wings of an Angel—*but you may be surprised to find out that the* Angel *is* You.

Acknowledgment

I would like to thank my partner, Michael "Harry" Hartmann, for all his support as this book was created. Although he constantly asked, "What are you smoking?" he still helped by taking a leap of faith that I knew exactly what I was doing.

Made in the USA
Charleston, SC
13 November 2013